SON OF THE SHOAH

Son of the Shoah

Poems from a Second-Generation Holocaust Survivor

Martin Herskovitz

Foreword by Judith Tydor Baumel-Schwartz

McFarland & Company, Inc., Publishers

Jefferson, North Carolina

ISBN (print) 978-1-4766-9978-3
ISBN (ebook) 978-1-4766-5825-4

LIBRARY OF CONGRESS CATALOGING DATA ARE AVAILABLE

Library of Congress Control Number 2025023110

Front cover images: family photographs from Herskovitz family collection;
gate of Auschwitz concentration camp and flower in Memorial to the Jews
of Europe in Berlin City, Germany © FSspolaor/EvrenKalinbacak /Shutterstock.

Printed in the United States of America

*McFarland & Company, Inc., Publishers
Box 611, Jefferson, North Carolina 28640
www.mcfarlandpub.com*

To Pearl

To my parents,
of blessed memory,
I can only hope that my kindness
is evident between the lines
of anger and pain.

To Amy Hudnall
whose efforts have given a voice to me
and my poetry in her endeavors to show
new perspectives of memory and trauma.
It is my hope that this book and her life work will
promote greater healing and understanding and
create a kinder and more compassionate world.

TABLE OF CONTENTS

Stories of Apostasy and Faith

Stories of Hope and Healing

FOREWORD

The Second Generation Finds Its Voice

Judith Tydor Baumel-Schwartz

Once upon a time there was no "Second Generation." There weren't even "Holocaust survivors." What we today call the "First Generation" or "Holocaust survivors" were more commonly known as "liberated Jews," "DPs," "refugees" and later, "immigrants." Only during the 1960s did the term "Holocaust survivor" become popular in the United States. After that time, their children were known as "children of survivors," having little independent identity other than being an appendage to their parents' wartime tribulations.

Slowly, however, these children began to take an identity of their own. The first "Second Generation" (2G) groups began to form in the mid–1970s as short-term awareness groups run by psychologists Bella Savran and Dr. Eva Fogelman at Boston University (1976), and then by Fogelman at the Hebrew University of Jerusalem (1978).[1] By then, they even had a name.

During the mid–1970s the term "Second Generation" and not just "Children of Survivors" had been coined, and was being

---

1. See also Eva Fogelman, "The Evolution of a Second-Generation of Holocaust Survivor Identity." 2017. Accessed April 22, 2025. https://evafogelman.com/publications/the-evolution-of-a-second-generation-holocaust-survivor-identity/.

used by the American Psychoanalytic Association.[2] Finally, they were viewed as an independent entity with its own identity, and not as an appendage to the survivors welcoming Fogelman to the annual meetings of their newly established "Group for the Psychoanalytic Study of the Effect of the Holocaust on the Second Generation,"[3] the members learned from her about the results of the short-term awareness groups, while emphasizing the significance behind the use of new nomenclature.

Second implies continuity, a continuation of survivor trauma, albeit in a different form. It also implies a connective chain and degree of dependence, as there is no "second" without "first." At the same time, it also gives expression to that generation's emerging adult identity and cohesion. No longer individual "children," but an entire generation with common denominators, stemming from its members' Holocaust heritage. Terminology is an important shaper of identity, and identity is the basis of being.

Interest in the Holocaust reached unparalleled heights following the broadcast of NBC's 1978 docudrama by that name,[4] and the publication of Helen Epstein's pathbreaking 2G introspection, *Children of the Holocaust*.[5] Bringing the topic of Holocaust survivors' descendants to the forefront, the first 2G Holocaust organizations began to crystallize in the United States and Israel. In November 1979, the First Conference of the Second Generation, held at Hebrew Union College, laid the groundwork for a 2G organization that would be established a year and a half later, following the World Gathering of Jewish Holocaust Survivors held in Jerusalem in June 1981. Although

---

2. American Psychoanalytic Association. https://apsa.org/.
3. Fogelman.
4. Herbert Brodkin, producer and Marvin J. Chomsky, director. *Holocaust* miniseries (NBC, 1978).
5. Helen Epstein, *Children of the Holocaust: Conversations with Sons and Daughters of Survivors* (New York: Penguin Books, 1988).

it was called "The International Network of Children of Jewish Holocaust Survivors" (INCJHS), it soon became a primarily American organization, headed by 2G activist and lawyer Menachem Rosensaft, son of post-war activists Josef and Dr. Hadassah Bimko-Rosensaft, a founding member of the United States Holocaust Memorial Council.

However, the first Israeli initiative to establish a 2G organization actually predated the American one. In March 1980, having heard about the American 2G conference, together with psychodrama specialist Ya'akov Naor, I founded the Irgun Yaldei Nitzolei Shoah Beyisrael—the Israeli Organization for Children of Holocaust Survivors, a long-named, short-lived body which lasted for less than six months due to discord over its organizational focus. Should its forty or so members devote their energies to hashing out personal fallout from their 2G background, or should they use that time to volunteer among elderly or indigent survivors? Were they meant to be a "rap (discussion) group," or devote themselves to social action? Could they do both?

Unable to reach a consensus, even between the organizers, the group disbanded a year before its American counterpart was established. Nevertheless, it heralded the creation of a larger Israeli 2G organization, Irgun Dor Hemshech Limoreshet Hashoah VeHagevurah (Second Generation Organization for the Legacy of Holocaust and Heroism) which, like the INCJHS, was also—unsurprisingly—formed in the wake of the 1981 World Gathering in Jerusalem. "The Second Generation will never know what the First Generation does in its bones, but what the Second Generation knows better than anyone else is the First Generation,"[6] writes 2G author and literary critic Melvin Bukiet. When survivors gather, their children are rarely far behind.

It was not by chance that both the American and the Israeli

---

6. Melvin Jules Bukiet, ed., *Nothing Makes You Free: Writings by Descendants of Jewish Holocaust Survivors* (New York: W.W. Norton, 2002).

2G national organizations were catalyzed by a Holocaust survivor conference and supported or partially initiated by survivor organizations of activists (including during the Holocaust) with organizational clout and financial resources. Finances "make or break" many organizations and 2G bodies suffered from chronic deficits. The backing of survivor organizations was often critical to their continued existence. Inevitably, the interconnection between survivors and 2G groups led to tacit power struggles between survivors wishing to see their legacy continue, and 2Gs determined to set their own path. Debates over policy and practice did not always end with hugs and smiles. Like families where children are considered adults only at middle age, it sometimes took a generational transition for 2Gs to come into their own.

"Second Generation" members worldwide may embody similar characteristics, but the same is not true of 2G organizations. It's not by chance that the major American and Israeli 2G organizations had different names stemming from the different Holocaust narratives and disparate natures of the survivor and 2G communities in those countries. While neither organization used the term "Second Generation," the American organization emphasized "Jewish" Holocaust Survivors, which in Israel was unnecessary. And although both groups had strong connections with Holocaust partisan organizations, only in Israel did the 2G organization's name refer to "Holocaust and Heroism" instead of "Holocaust," reflecting the prevalent Israeli Statist[7] terminology and narrative.

Another difference was geographical. At an early stage the American and Israeli 2G endeavors took on different trajectories, influenced by geography and organizational culture. The sheer geographical vastness of the United States and a tradition of

---

7. A statist position is the one that believes that economic controls and planning should be concentrated in a highly centralized government.

decentralization encouraged the development of local 2G groups throughout the country. These flourished in cities such as Atlanta, Cleveland, Detroit, Los Angeles, Miami, New York, Philadelphia, San Francisco, St. Louis, Teaneck, and Washington, D.C., from the mid–1980s onward. Some groups were connected to the INC-JHS, while others began as an existing Holocaust-related organization such as WAGRO, the Warsaw Ghetto Uprising organization,[8] whose members were acutely aware of the aging process and wished to create reserves for the future.

Second Generation organizations in Israel developed somewhat differently as circumscribed geographical parameters precluded the need to develop local 2G groups. During the early 1980s, the Israeli national Dor Hemschech organization, whose members met in the greater Tel Aviv area, included several dozen 2G activists from all over the country. Financial difficulties having to do with publications and mailing plagued the organization, and it concentrated on national conferences and promoted Holocaust-related educational activity. It did not sponsor psychological discussion groups like those of the local American 2G organizations, possibly because of its being an Israeli organization (neither did the American national organization) or because of the different cultural attitude in Israel of the 1980s towards self-awareness groups. Most of its efforts were devoted to public conferences, and towards the end of the decade, it became active in promoting educational missions to Poland and supporting the March of the Living,[9] initiated in 1988.

---

8. On April 19, 1943, the Warsaw Ghetto Uprising erupted when German troops attempted to empty the ghetto of all Jewish inhabitants. Fought by approximately 7,000 Jewish Ghetto fighters, the uprising was the largest in Holocaust history and lasted for almost a full month. It ended in their defeat.

9. The March of the Living was first held in 1988 and continues to this day. Its goal is to provide an "annual educational program brining individuals from around the world to Poland and Israel to study the Holocaust and examine the roots of prejudice, intolerance and hatred." "International March of the Living," https://www.motl.org/about/.

As survivors everywhere recognized that their biological clock was ticking, 2G sections were also being formed in Israeli-based survivor organizations and *Landsmanschaften* such as the Organization of Jews from Salonika, the Association of Jews from Bochnia, and the She'erit Hapletah—Bergen Belsen Organization—in Israel. The relationship between the survivors and 2Gs in all these frameworks throughout the world was often fraught with undercurrents, recalling those between survivors and their children everywhere.

New Stages in 2G and 3G Organizational Identity

From the mid–1990s onward, a new stage began in 2G organizational development propelled by generational transitions and technological developments. Two of its catalysts were the understanding that the First Generation was aging and would slowly disappear, a factor that would change the lives of their children and transfer the commemorative process to them. The second was the growth of the internet, making mailing issues a problem of the past and enabling 2G groups to use that platform in order to connect.

One result was the creation of online 2G communities, the first of which was known as the 2nd-Gen. [Mailing] List.[10] Begun in 1995, the "List" was the brainchild of Paul Foldes, a 2G electrical engineer and consumer attorney turned businessman, who hadn't been able to find a face-to-face group in the Washington, D.C., area where he lived. Knowing that online communities were an opportunity to reach beyond local meetings, he founded the List even before the web existed.

---

10. Details regarding the 2nd-Gen. Mailing List can be found at: https://remember.org/2g.html.

As an internet-based group, the List bypassed certain problems that face-to-face 2G groups had grappled with. It was the first to break local and national barriers to become a truly international, English-speaking 2G framework. Unlike 2G face-to-face organizations, it required no funding. Freed from having to pander to various groups for financial support, its active members could devote their energies to their favorite 2G activities: discussing their past and arguing about their present and future. Ultimately succumbing to internet ills such as flaming, trolling, and cyberbullying, the List went through several metamorphoses by which time I was already an active member. Meanwhile, suffering from moderator burnout, its founder and some active members eventually left not only their moderating positions, but the group. The List was also affected by platform instability, forced to migrate from one free platform to another until I eventually turned it into a Google group that I administer (but don't moderate), where it functions today.

As the List celebrated a decade of existence, Facebook was born, offering another platform for 2G encounters. Since then, a plethora of 2G Facebook groups have been created to disseminate information about Holocaust-related and 2G events, share experiences, and focus on specific issues such as 2Gs obtaining European citizenship. While perusing the numerous English-language Facebook groups created for descendants of Holocaust survivors, one is struck by their vast geographical, political, and social diversity. American political ideologies, attitudes towards European governments, particularly those in Eastern Europe, and debates over the policies of the State of Israel are a few of the more common topics that surface continuously on some groups to become acrimonious discussions.

Certain groups are public, others are closed. Some allow free expression; others ask members to refrain from making political statements of any kind. Some boast thousands of members, while others have only a handful. Some become platforms for what is facetiously known as the "Suffering Olympics," comparing who among their members endured more as a 2G, while others only discuss educational matters. Many of these groups, including "the 2nd-Gen List," became a lifeline for 2Gs during the Covid-19 pandemic when face-to-face meetings often came to an abrupt halt.

The internet's international nature and characteristics of becoming a great equalizer has enabled English-speaking (or reading) Israelis to actively participate in international 2G online groups. A quarter of the members of the List live in Israel. One of them is Martin Herskovitz, the author of this book.

Creative Endeavors of the Second Generation

One of the added benefits of having members of the Second Generation becoming more aware of what they had experienced was the fact that some of them turned to the creative arts in order to express their feelings, fears and hopes about being 2G. Some chose art, music, writing, or plastic arts as a full-time profession. Others preferred to develop their creative expressions alongside other lines of work. There were those who had always felt the creative spark while some, like Martin Herskovitz, only realized that need in themselves after joining a 2G group in which they expressed themselves for the first time as children of survivors.

In his essay "An Essay on Cultural Criticism and Society" (1949),[11] the eminent German philosopher Theodor Adorno stated that "after Auschwitz, to write a poem is barbaric,"

---

11. Theodor W. Adorno, "An Essay on Cultural Criticism and Society." In *Prisms: Essays on Veblen, Huxley, Benjamin, Bach, Proust, Schoenberg, Spengler Jazz, Kafka* (University of Pennsylvania, 1967), pp. 19–34, http://direct.mit.edu/books/book/chapter-pdf/157614/9780262266840_cae.pdf.

which is often misquoted as "one can no longer write poems after Auschwitz." Yet all the poetry, and especially that written by 2Gs, that has been written since Auschwitz proves both statements to be incorrect.

One example is the collection of poems in this book, written by Martin Herskovitz. Son of a Holocaust survivor, Herskovitz's powerful and poignant poems give readers a sense of what it was like to grow up as a member of that very special Second Generation. Some of the poems express profound sadness; others great hope. Various poems allow readers to step into the author's mind and heart; another group keeps them at arm's length while allowing them to receive a whiff of what it was like to live in a 2G household and to build a 2G home. Each of the poems is special. Together, they comprise an unforgettable collection of thoughts, memories, dreams, and hopes.

As a Holocaust historian, my way of expressing my 2G heritage was to research and write historical essays and books about the Holocaust and its aftermath, including the world of the Second and Third (and today even Fourth) generations. Written from the heart, my historical writing must nevertheless conform to a professional template that places facts, and not personal impressions or emotions such as fears and hopes, at the forefront.

On the other end of the scale from history are the creative arts. As a poet, Martin Herskovitz has the advantage of not being limited by such templates. Freed from such limitations, he can express his feelings, which are embedded in every poem in this collection. Marty and I have been friends for years, and I have read his poetry for over two decades, watching it develop and grow richer and deeper with the passage of time. Like a good wine, age is often beneficial to poets, allowing them to sense and describe new dimensions of their experiences and feelings which rise to the surface as the years go by. Such is the nature of the book you are reading and the poetry that follows this Foreword. Heady as a mature wine and steeped in the emotions of a 2G with many years of life experience, the author looks back at his life with experienced eyes and ever-developing creative powers. For me, reading this collection of 2G poetry has been an unforgettable experience, and I hope that it will be so for you as well.

Judith Tydor Baumel-Schwartz
Ramat Gan, January 2025

Bibliography

Adorno, Theodor W. "An Essay on Cultural Criticism and Society," pp. 19–34. In *Prisms: Essays on Veblen, Huxley, Benjamin, Bach, Proust, Schoenberg, Spengler Jazz, Kafka*. Philadelphia: University of Pennsylvania, 1967. http://direct.mit.edu/books/book/chapter-pdf/157614/9780262266840_cae.pdf.

American Psychoanalytic Association. Accessed April 22, 2025. https://apsa.org/.

Brodkin, Herbert, producer, and Marvin J. Chomsky, director. *Holocaust* Miniseries, NBC, 1978.

Bukiet, Melvin Jules, ed. *Nothing Makes You Free: Writings by Descendants of Jewish Holocaust Survivors*. New York: W.W. Norton, 2002.

Epstein, Helen. *Children of the Holocaust: Conversations with Sons and Daughters of Survivors*. New York: Penguin Books, 1988.

Fogleman, Eva. "The Evolution of a Second-Generation of Holocaust Survivor Identity." 2017. Accessed April 22, 2025. https://evafogelman.com/publications/the-evolution-of-a-second-generation-holocaust-survivor-identity/.

March of the Living. "International March of the Living." Accessed April 22, 2025. https://www.motl.org/about/.

Judith Tydor Baumel-Schwartz is the director of the Arnold and Leona Finkler Institute of Holocaust Research, the Abraham and Edita Spiegel Family Professor in Holocaust Research, the Rabbi Pynchas Brener Professor in Research on the Holocaust of European Jewry, and a professor of Modern Jewish History in the Israel and Golda Koschitzky Department of Jewish History and Contemporary Jewry at Bar-Ilan University. She is also the consulting historian and curator at the Museum of Jewish Heritage in New York.

INTRODUCTION

My Journey to Remembrance

My house was too fierce a place to ever serve as a home. First, there were too many walls. Barriers were everywhere; communication was impossible. Second, despite all these walls, our house never really provided shelter, as if the home had no roof. I felt exposed, vulnerable, and unsafe. I don't blame my parents for trying to build a home and failing. My mother was a Holocaust survivor. My father was left to live with his grandparents when his parents and three other siblings (one older sister, two younger) immigrated to America. These traumas which were foisted on them prevented them from creating a true home for us. They were able to build only a shell of a home that left us without a true anchor to build our lives.

For me, being a Second Generation survivor, a son of the Shoah, has been a modern-day Mark of Cain. I have been unable, as I have imagined my father also being unable, to find a true feeling of belonging, of finding my place. My life is a constant search for looking to belong, and at the same time running away from belonging, terrified of being abandoned.

A child of Holocaust survivors seldom has a life of their own. We are almost always named for someone, or more usually, more than one person and we are brought into the world to replace those souls who were lost, dozens of souls.

The path of my life was determined before I was born. I was born as an attempt to fix all that had been broken. If I could have done a good enough job to replace them, then my parents wouldn't have to ever think about those others, would be able to pretend that they needn't be mourned. It was an impossible task, and I failed miserably. I was born for one reason, and one reason only, and I failed.

In the mid–'90s, I started to read everything I could about the psychopathology of being a child of a Holocaust survivor. In my Internet surfing, I came across a lot of interesting information. In one of the sites I visited in the year 1999, I found, as Judy explained in her Foreword, the Second Generation (2G) List.

I joined the List and started corresponding with the List members. I don't remember any names or the issues we discussed. What I do remember is how emotionally affected I was by the discussions and how safe I felt discussing them. It was a secure place where I could discuss any of my emotional issues. Problems I had regarded as exclusively mine were now the very same issues others discussed.

The thoughts I shared and my responses to the disclosures of others took the form of verse. Poetry was the easiest way for me to express the intended emotions I was feeling at the time. My poetry came from the heart, I didn't know if it was good. But it was real. The others encouraged me; they said it was good. To me it didn't matter, I had things buried deep inside that I had to say, and I believed if I said them, then perhaps I could heal.

My poetry became a way for my inner child to voice his feelings, thoughts and emotions. As a Second Generation survivor, I am uncomfortable expressing these feelings because they are often an indictment of my parents. They had suffered too much pain, and it is not their fault that the Holocaust destroyed something within them. And I regret that. But these feelings burn within me, and I know they existed then because they exist in me now in my most intimate relationships. But if I can heal myself and feel the love inside of me, then I can connect with my parents' love which, perhaps, did exist but I was too impaired until now to feel it.

The creative process allowed me a safe place in which to vent my frustration and anger, allowed me the cathartic experience I required to process and resolve my childhood trauma. The process of catharsis, dialogue, and reconciliation that was started on the List provided me a path to healing that has continued since. Poetry functions as a form of expression and protest, to communicate and to grieve, to vent and to comfort, and ultimately, it serves as an expression of change and hope. It is from the seeds of early poems long ago that this book has sprouted.

It is my wish and hope that readers find some comfort and healing in my words. There is much suffering in the world, too many people have suffered too much trauma, and I hope that this expression of my trauma and my family's trauma will resonate with others and perhaps help them in their journey to healing.

Stories
of Forgetting
and Re-Remembering

ECLIPSE

How did I know about the Holocaust
amidst the silence,
or was the knowing encrypted on my soul,
trickling, in time, to my consciousness.
Perhaps the angel Gabriel[12] taught me the
    entire Torah of the Shoah
in my Mother's womb,
then touched my upper lip
and disappeared.
An awareness that is never taught,
can never be unlearned,
can never be forgotten.

---

12. In Jewish tradition it is believed that an angel teaches all of the Torah to an infant in utero. When the child is born, it forgets everything he or she had known when the angel touches the child above the lips. The touch creates the vertical groove between the upper lip and the nose.

Unknown/Unowned

If,
as the Rabbis say,
each life has a meaning,
then each death should have its meaning too.
A tear, a shiver
a murmur
of Blessed Memory
after a name,
even just a glimpse of a memory,
like the flicker of a lamp.
But a death unmourned,
unnoted
is a cruelty that never should have been created,
it is a cruelty beyond flames,
beyond dust.

Unmourned

It is a time of mourning in Israel,
grandparents mourn their grandchildren,
and children, their parents.
An entire country versed in mourning
except for me.
My grandparents hold their faces earthbound
to catch some of the tears,
tears they have never known,
for all died with them,
except the few who refuse to remember,
so as to go on.
But I, who have never known their embrace,
cannot mourn instead,
but their pain, akin to mine,
we share,
which will have to suffice,
as yet.
It is a time of mourning
and I sit among the unmourned.

PHOTOGRAPHS

1

My great uncle Haim Stern returned to Seredne[13] after the war,
took the key from the neighbor,
to return shortly,
a shoebox under his arm.
He strode toward the tree grove.
The bonfire in the grove burnt the photographs well
as he stood over the curling pictures, prodding them deeper
into the flames,
the nitrate smoke chafing his eyes.
He sat in the clearing till the embers died down,
then freed, left for America,
his spare set of shoes now in the shoebox.
2
My father has put away the pictures from before the war and
he can't find them.
What good are those pictures, he says, they were all blurry
and in the posed pictures they all look like statues.
Better we should take pictures of our wonderful grandchildren,
not blurry and in color.
Much better.
3
I don't have any pictures of my uncles who died in Auschwitz.

---

13. Seredne/Serednje is a village that exists in present-day Ukraine. It was established in the Middle Ages.

My Uncle Meshulam died when he was 4 years old.
I would feel pretty silly holding a picture of a four year old
and saying this is my uncle.
It is hard for me to imagine that I had a family at all.
I'm not a god that can create a family
out of motes of dust.

SILENCE

My mother has never spoken of what happened during the
   War,
her silence unsullied
"Just look on the Internet,"
she says.
"It is full of stories
no different than mine."
Only silence is truly hers.

Tears

The souls of the dead lie dormant
under the filmy wrapping of the years
in anticipation
like a child who hides beneath a blanket waits
to be discovered.
Our cries of protest do not move them
nor do our tears of indignation,
they huddle tighter at the bolts of anger.
But when we whisper their names
and cry tears of longing that they have yet to know,
then the warmth of the tears caresses their foreheads
and they blink open their eyes,
astonished,
and stir themselves, loosening their limbs,
to fly down to our dreams.

Yom Kippur Eve[14]

I take out the family tree
of the names I know
and of the nameless.
No one seems to know
how many children Chaim Stern had
from before the Holocaust.
Some of the people I think I recognize,
some will remain unknown for eternity.
Because, after I asked,
my mother would wake
hours before dawn,
rattling the tea kettle in the kitchen.
I just take out the list,
to ask for their forgiveness,
for my ignorance,
for their anonymity,
but I did the best I could
and I can't regret that.
And if they can forgive,
then they can also love
and know the responsibility of being loved.
So maybe they can understand,
I ask for that.

---

14. Yom Kippur is the holiest holiday in the Jewish faith. It is also known as the
Day of Atonement and is centered on repentance and atonement.

Because on Yom Kippur the High Priest
sacrificed two goats,
one for his family
And another, the scapegoat[15]
for them,
the forgotten.
There are supposed to be two
and I am but one.

---

15. On the Day of Atonement, according to the biblical text of Leviticus, a pair of kid goats are chosen by the high priest. One is the scapegoat, and it takes on all of the Israelite's sins and impurities and is then released into the wilderness. The scapegoat represents the removal of all sins. The other kid is sacrificed to God.

Names

My mother's father was named Mordechai Kleinbart.
But maybe, because he was the eldest son,
his mother called him Tateleh,
and his father probably called him Mordkhe
like my father called me.
His sister and brothers called him, perhaps, Moti,
except for the baby sister who called him Momo,
even after she grew up.
His wife's cousins at the winery may have called him Kleiny,
and his children surely called him Tati,
as did his wife,
except late at night, alone in the bedroom,
she would maybe call to him with Yiddish[16] familiars
in a soft erotic lilt.
Or maybe not.
Because Mordechai Kleinbart is the single name I have
and it alone is carved into stone
and molded into bronze.
All the other names exist only in memories long interred
or pages yet to be written.

---

16. Yiddish is a West Germanic language spoken by Ashkenazi Jews. Originating in the 9th century, it is a blend of German and Hebrew. It is still spoken today in enclaves of Ashkenazi Jews around the world.

Names and Stories

Some of us have only names.
Names are good for reading at memorial services
and putting on bronze plaques in the synagogue
next to a flickering bulb,
which is almost as good as mourning.
Some of us have stories without names,
names removed like fangs
so that they cannot wound.
So I am destined to tell the story over and over again,
unsatisfied.
Sometimes I feel like putting the names in column A
and the stories in column B,
like the test we took in grade school:
1. George Washington and
c. first President of the United States,
Connecting the story and the name.
And on Remembrance Day[17] I can feel I am mourning a real
    person,
not just a name with no history
or a story without a name,
and I can hope that the tears begin to fall.
But if I have erred,

---

17. International Holocaust Remembrance Day was set aside by the United Nations to remember the events of the Holocaust. It occurs annually on January 27. The day was chosen because it was the day Auschwitz-Birkenau was freed by the Russians in 1945.

then I have mourned a fiction,
a phantom who existed only in my manipulations
and I have wasted the day.
Or do the dead know how to lift the tears
from the page on which they have fallen
and carry them in cupped palms
to their proper page.

MINTS

When I asked about her grandfather,
my mother said he gave his grandchildren mints,
then silence.
Not if the mints were azure blue
or pinwheel red and white,
not the peppery scent of their breaths,
not of the toddler's cries because he would not get,
just mints.
It is left for me to imagine my uncles crunching impatiently
the hard candy when they tired of letting it dissolve,
as I would, a generation on.

ERGO SUM

The relatives who died "in the war"
have faded in and out of our lives,
not alive, not even the littlest bit alive,
but then not dead,
gone or lost in the war.
Maybe once or twice mentioned as dead or killed,
but this is stated
with such dispassion
that it seems not true.
So I am going to Auschwitz
to give them life,
to find them within the ledgers and the Lagers
within the piles of shoes,
within the ashes.
For you cannot be destroyed unless you were once alive,
so within the desolation I will prove their existence,
like a latter-day Descartes,
"You were killed,
therefore you were,"
and I will grieve.

INEFFABLE

In the face of the ineffable
there can be no words,
they say,
only silence.
But my life has been measured by decades of silence,
not mere kilometers.
So the crunch of flagstones,
the swirl of winds,
even the tears
are no stead.
Here in Auschwitz, silence will not suffice,
for when words return,
they return as they were,
like seeds scattered on the frozen ground.
But if a voice can rise from the destruction,
to parse therewith a syntax of the pain,
then words entombed shall resurgent flow,
words whose tears may heal the soul again.

Four Sons[18]

After the redemption there were four sons,
so too after the destruction.
The wise son pores over tractates of names,
and lists of towns, too small, it would seem,
to bear the burden of its dead.
The simple son stares at photographs on museum walls,
and is visited at night by the visages of the dead,
who awaken him with tears.
The son who knows not to ask,
awaits the day the silence is broken.
The evil son...
after the destruction, there is no evil son,
just a son who yearns to be normal,
and believes that, by forgetting the past,
he might be like others.

---

18. In Jewish tradition, the "Four Sons" or the four children of the Seder refers
to four different personalities, each with a unique approach to the Passover Seder.
It represents the different levels of understanding and engagement with Jewish tra-
dition. These four perspectives derive from four passages of the Torah that instruct
on the story of Passover. Passover is a major Jewish holiday that celebrates the Exo-
dus of the Israelites from slavery in Egypt. The Seder is a traditional Passover meal
and ritual to commemorate this Exodus. The four personalities are the Wise Son,
the Wicked Son, the Simple Son, and the Son Who Doesn't Know How to Ask.

Stories of Solutions
and Dissolutions

Renewal

Jerusalem after the snow,
almond trees blanketed in frost,
I watched their branches swirl in the gusts,
showering petals to the ground
that could not hold fast.
It is cruel to bloom in the winter,
when one's sap is turgid and sour,
exposing small translucent blossoms just born
to the shivering sleet.
What fruits will be brought forth from these,
thick husked and bitter no doubt.
And when stillness comes,
of what do these blossoms dream?
Of warm summer breezes and shimmering red flowers,
and hummingbirds craning their sparkling neck
to sip of their fragrant nectar, perhaps.
But theirs is to bloom while the hummingbirds sleep,
impelled by some impassive force of nature,
bent on renewal,
to put forth these tiny, pale flowers
in the midst of the maelstrom.

BERRIES

I remember the ceremony, as a child,
in the lengthening shade of the mulberry tree,
as the kibbutz[19] elders read the names.
Their names,
names now ours.
Names like a breeze
that wafted upwards through the tendrilled
green mulberries.
Names like the shadow that grew long
with the day's end.
Late that summer I would return to the tree
to pick these mulberries from the ground,
their sweetness bittered with dust,
unaware of the names
that had lodged in my soul
like the tiny hard seeds of a mulberry.

---

19. A kibbutz is a collective settlement in Israel usually based on communal living and agriculture, shared resources and a focus on equality and cooperation.

RUNES

When I was a toddler,
two and a half or so,
I learned about a room fan,
with my fingers
between the slats,
as children, left alone, tend to do.
Sixty-seven stitches later
the back of my left hand
has been inscribed with these pale runes,
glyphs by which I guide my life.
Deciphered:
Do not need.
Do not want.
Do not love too much,
and you will not be wounded.

Snow Queen

When I was five,
I was terrified
that the Snow Queen,
whiteness and ice,
would kidnap me to her Arctic castle.
While other kids feared vampires and monsters
with fangs that gnashed and chomped,
I was terrified of cold blue eyes
and of being whisked away.

THE FOURTH CANDLE

I wake from my Friday afternoon nap,
My mother beside me, weeping silently.
She leads me by the hand.
"Come, Tati has gone to shul,
it is time to light the candles.
One for Tati, one for you, one for me,"
and one unnamed, for the silence.
Then dabbing away the streaks of tears,
the Sabbath Queen[20] should see no sadness,
we sit on cane-backed chairs at the table
to wait for Father to return.
Today I do not mourn.
But some nights I sprinkle a few drops
on my pillow
to lay upon the moistness
and dream.

---

20. The Sabbath Queen or Shabbat Queen is a metaphorical term referring to the Sabbath day. The Sabbath is often referred to as a bride or queen and anticipates the holiness of the day of rest, the Sabbath.

ESCAPE

You loved me like an escaped prisoner,
glancing to the sides,
never at me,
your subjugator, once again
recreating the nightmare world
of madness and captivity.
So I was exiled to a side room
to lie on a thin striped blanket
and you returned to your chores,
you, enmeshed in anguish,
and I, in solitude.

Pharaoh's Cows[21]

I am part of a war unfinished,
a war that can never be finished,
for its corpses remain unburied,
its dead unmourned.
I am a character in a narrative never told,
a syllable in a secret left unwhispered,
its message conveyed in silence,
enrobed in secrecy.
I have spent my life peering into
the chasms of your need,
hungers unsated, hungers never to be sated,
like Pharaoh's cows,
a voracity that devours fatted heifers,
ever gaunt.

21. The biblical story of Joseph prophesying the Pharaoh's dream of seven cows
was thought to be from God and a warning to prepare for famine.

ROOTLESSNESS

My father, aged twelve
arrived in America,
seven years after his family,
left him in Seredne.
Upon his arrival, he refused to kiss the unfamiliar woman
who met him at the pier,
his mother.
I imagine that, until he got readjusted to his new family,
that he felt between homes, rootless.
His eyes would lose their focus every once in a while
like they did as a five year old,
trying to imagine his mother,
until he made himself grow up quickly
and deny his need for a mother at all.
I think about my father's legacy,
wandering alone,
contemplating,
how much of a home
I can learn not to need
and how much of a home
I will be able to build.

HOUSE KEYS

I used to lose my keys to the house a lot,
once, they fell through the grate of the sewer
and once down the manhole cover
next to Yad Vashem.
And my mother asked me:
Why did you lose them?
And why so many times?
And I had no answer.
So we both stood over the manhole
without words,
waiting for someone to come by
to salvage them and us.

Isaac

I have had no great test to endure
as Abraham[22] prevailed the fire and the wrath.
Only the silent binding to the altar,
the resoluteness of his sacrifice
despite my quiet tears.
I am deemed to be symbol,
allowed no pain.
So I remain in the field
distant, apart
until Rebecca[23] comes to lead me to her tent
and lays my head upon her breast
and I sleep.

---

22. Abraham is a foundational figure in Judaism, Christianity and Islam. He is considered the "father of the faithful."
23. Rebecca is the wife of Isaac in the Bible and is a prominent Jewish matriarch.

ARARAT[24]

"And sometimes memory is the sea that covers everything
Like a flood, and oblivion is a dry land that saves like
Ararat"—Yehuda Amichai[25]

I have no childhood memories,
perhaps forgetting is my redemption
from traumas I can only surmise.
Adrift, like Noah,
on an endless sea of gray,
waiting to be redeemed.
Like Noah, naked,
dislodged from grace,
I curse and bless my sons, in turn
and dream that I might ride the wind unto a rainbow
golden, crimson and blue.

---

24. Located in eastern Turkey, Ararat is considered the location of Noah's Ark and the most sacred space for Armenians.

25. Yehuda Amichai is considered one of Israel's finest poets.

FULL AND EMPTY

I am a man of fullness.
Full bodied.
Full of regrets,
full of flaws
that I call eccentricities.
Overflowing with clothes that no longer fit,
that I am unable to throw away.
I have check stubs from 29 years ago.
I am also empty.
I am missing the spoon from the Merchant Marines
that my father left behind,
the white stuffed lamb that I held in my first photograph,
smiling.
The kippah[26] that my wife crocheted for me when we got
    married
for under the wedding canopy.
Most of the important papers and people
tend to evaporate somehow.
I even managed to lose a dog.
Even my luggage disappeared once.
I find it is hard to hold on to things,
And even harder to get rid of them.

---

26. Kippah means "dome" in Hebrew, and it is a word for the cover men wear on
their heads. In Yiddish it is known as yarmulka.

UNWEPT

I tried to be angry with them,
because of my misery,
but could not.
You see Hitler and Eichmann,[27] not they, were guilty.
My pain remained unspoken,
our bond, desolate.
So when the time came to grieve,
I stood silent by their graves,
in the valley of a thousand stones,
I was but another.

---

27. Adolf Eichmann was an officer in the Nazi Party who helped organize the Holocaust through the Wannsee Conference and elsewhere.

Sitting Shiva

"Mother knows best,"
people said,
and I nodded.
She nurtured me,
nourished me,
worried about me,
and she was even proud of me,
if only furtively.
but she also ignored me,
distrusted
And resented me, although she never said this aloud.
She never ever hugged me
or said she loved me.
She sent me far away
and never bothered for my return.
I never really confided in her,
nor she to me.
A mother like Schrödinger's cat,[28]
a mother and a not-mother all at once,
with no window.

---

28. Schrödinger's Cat is a famous thought experiment that demonstrates the idea of quantum physics.

Life's Delights

They say about us, the 2gs,
that we don't know how to have fun.
But I am delighted to find a forgotten container
of cottage cheese
in the back of the refrigerator,
a little tangy but still good.
And I find joy in the slightly tattered chair that the neighbors
    had thrown away.
And I love to eat the leftovers from my grandchildren's plate
and to give the bones to the dog,
to see his tail sway.
I revel in the quiet after the grandchildren have finally left.
There is much to celebrate,
finding a dollar bill in the gutter,
lunching on free samples at the supermarket.
Or even just a day that passes by
without demands.

Stories of Attachments
and Abandonments

A Love Poem

You say I don't love you.
I love you no differently than my parents
loved me.
Isn't that love?
Neither of us knows.
Love has no formula
that can be held to the light.
I feel what I felt
when my parents cared for me,
as they could.
Is that love?
Or are they impaired,
am I impaired,
so that what I grasped
was too full of holes
to be anything real?
You say I don't hug you,
I will hold on more.
You say I don't care enough or care too much,
I will cherish you, more or less.
You say I shout,
from now on I will whisper.
The problem isn't proving to you my love
but in convincing myself.

CLOWNS

We are both amateurs at love,
impersonating intimacy
attempting to be Ozzie and Harriet
or Donna Reed and her husband
(did he even have a name?)
A Purim masquerade[29] of a marriage
in which we disguised ourselves
as we attempted to sing songs of love,
tone deaf
with no notes,
Chiribim, Chiribum.[30]

---

29. Purim is a joyous Jewish holiday celebrating Jewish survival. It is known for feasting, costumes and masquerades.
30. The name of a Jewish folksong.

Intimacy

I cannot contain your needs
when you are near me,
when you are close
I feel inadequate.
Distance yourself from me
and I can mold the remembrance of you
into a shape I can contain
and love.
When you are near
all I manage is to silence
the static that crackles in my mind,
quiescence, not love.
Go from me
so that I can love you,
the distance shelters me,
and allows me
my stealthed love.

Spilled Milk

I am one who seeks intimacy
in desperate places,
because I was born into a family of disconnection,
unwilling to bask in the other,
afraid to ask of the other.
In our family, we don't lament over people who are gone,
preferring to move on,
choosing not to cry over substances spilt.

DEPARTURES

I am going to a writing workshop
at the Eternal Life Synagogue
to write about my father.
Which is doubly ironic,
because my dad is dead for a decade and a half
and because,
even when alive,
we never had much room for the other in our lives,
let alone eternally.
So I am going there to write and perhaps to grieve
for the relationship we had
and hadn't,
and how sometimes it is difficult
to tell the difference
between leave-taking and desertion.

FIRST LOVE

I loved her at a time
when I felt unloved,
unlovable,
when everyone but her offered advice, not support,
proposing change in my world of flux,
when I yearned for stability.
But my want was dagger-sharp and deep
and its wounds were found in her reticence,
in her downturned eyes.
So I distanced myself while there was still love to cherish,
a mere shimmering on the horizon,
but I seek it yet,
in the reunifications of life,
of hotel lobbies and airport terminals,
with bouquet laden arms.
I delight in the wonder of reconnection,
and mourn the enchantment that has faded,
a love flown, never to recur.

I Wound

I was wounded,
I am wounded,
I wound.
It need not be inevitable, I suppose.
For the fortunate, there is healing,
I was wounded, but am no longer.
But even in the absence of healing,
one can choose to not cause pain:
I am wounded but will not wound,
or in the words of Hillel the Elder,[31]
what is hateful to you,
refrain from doing to another.
Painfully simple,
facile like a third-grader's scrawled
"I will not disturb in class,"
50 times.
But what is hateful is nearest,
what is hateful is familiar,
what is hateful rises to the fore.

---

31. Hillel the Elder was a Jewish religious leader, scholar and sage. His is attributed with developing the Mishnah and the Talmud.

VULNERABILITY

Her mother away,
the child spoke on the phone,
and her voice cracked,
"I miss you."
And through the crack spilled
the vulnerability and the fear
as if she might fall.
Recovering,
she straightened herself,
closing the rift,
smiling with glistening eyes.
It reminded me of children past
tutored to be impervious,
criss-crossing the cracks
with layer upon layer,
until nothing showed,
sturdying the wall
against the churning inside
with eyes that dared not glisten.

Rooster from Seredne

I once said that I had no photographs from
"Before the War."
That is not exactly true.
We have a photograph of a rooster strutting
in my great grandfather's yard.
It belongs to my six year daughter now.
She calls it "her rooster from Seredne."
On cold winter nights
when she awakens
and I have yet to sleep,
I sit on the edge of her bed
and ask her to tell me the story
of the rooster from Seredne.
But she dozes back to sleep
instead.

Stories of Desolation
and Solace

My Mother's
Unspoken Memories

In the aftermath of the Holocaust, we were told:
Remember what the Nazis did to us,
remember how they all stood by.
Never Again.
Large lessons.
But Mother, where are the tiny memories?
The memories that must have been, but never spoken—
Of shivering from cold and fatigue.
Of propping up your sick sister at roll call,
the suffocating summer dust in the brick factory in Ungvar,[32]
the moan of the old man as he died on the train to Auschwitz,
the embarrassment of seeing your mother stripped to the bone,
the strange sensation of your shaven head,
the suddenness of how quickly your world disintegrated,
and how quickly you adapted to an appalling, new reality.
The particles of ashes in the air,
the chill that stayed from October to May,
the everpresent yearning,
the knowledge that, even if you were to survive,
you will never be made whole again.

---

32. Ungvar is thought to be a village in areas where Hungarians and Czechs
fought one another during World War II.

PIXIEMAN

They called him Pixieman
because his forehead sloped up in a funny way and
he laughed a lot.
His shoes were laced with thick twine
whose bows would flop with every step.
On the streets of Seredne,
the little children would run in his wake
and tease him,
"Pixieman, Pixieman," they would yell
but he would just smile.
When the Nazis marshalled them to the edge of the village,
he bolted in panic into the forest.
A dozen soldiers were sent
while the rest of the town had to wait facing forward.
Out of corner of her eye, my aunt saw him being dragged,
sobbing and shivering back into the line.
Pixieman shuffling forward,
his shoelaces caked in mud,
tears flowed down his cheeks,
trembling.

HISTORY

My mother has no history,
only labyrinths of possible realities.
"What if, on the causeway,
we had pulled Hensche with us,
and piled her a mound of gravel on which to stand,
propping her between our shoulders,
pinching her when the officer neared
to stand erect.
She might have lived."
But instead my Mother and her sister sent her to the other side
to help with the children huddled about their Mother.
"We didn't know, we couldn't know."
But even so, could they have dragged Hensche from her fate,
or would she have plunged the other three
together with her, into the void?
For in a place where death is imminent,
and survival a chance occurrence,
there is no surety, there is surely no surety,
and destiny vexed turns easily vengeful.
The paths not taken in Auschwitz are never green or
overgrown,
but alleyways of blackest cinder,
jagged and rough.
My mother visits these passages in her fantasies,
bowing her head before the torment.

Seder Night,
1944 Birkenau

The firstborn of Velvel and Feige Gruen was spared on Passover
    Eve 5704,[33]
But all her brothers and sisters were killed.
The firstborn of Lipa and Masha Tarnowicz was spared on
    Passover Eve 5704,
but thousands of others strode to their deaths.
Why the terrible deliverance of that night?
Why did the Angel of Death just stay, just stay?
Was it that their prayers were whispered and not cried aloud.
Or that there was no hyssop in Auschwitz 1944,
and no blood,
just ashes and smoke.

---

33. This date reflects the Hebrew calendar which is based on a lunisolar calendar
and is the official calendar of Israel.

PROVINCES

I went on a tour of the camps with Yad Vashem[34]
"to the Provinces of Persecution."[35]
We visited three camps where the victims were murdered,
and four camps in which they were not murdered, but
died from disease and starvation.
We walked along the paths where they marched and died,
and we visited forests where they lay in ditches and were shot.
We visited towns with no Jews
and synagogues without penitents.
But in all these places,
my family,
clung to life,
and planned a future that never came to be,
exchanging recipes soon to be prepared,
that remain uncooked.
They stood ramrod straight during roll call
so as not to be chosen.
Even when weakened,
they continued to dream dreams
to cling to life.
as death drew ever closer.

---

34. Yad Vashem is Israel's official memorial/museum/education center to honor
victims of the Holocaust. It is considered one of the most important sites for learn-
ing and memory of the Holocaust in the world.
35. This phrase usually refers to places where religious people have faced perse-
cution.

But we visited places with none of this vitality, merely the pallor of death.

MEMENTO

I had wanted to bring a memento from Auschwitz
with which to remember those who died.
I picked up a fragment of brick, remembering that
Esther, a survivor had said that, if their mouths
were not too parched,
they would moisten these,
to rub them on their cheeks,
the harsh ochre masking the pallor beneath
to survive the day.

MISSING PERSONS

She would sit alone in her room after school,
practicing her cursive to be round, not spiky
until Mother came home.
She'd wait for her Mother to lie on the couch,
draping a damp towel over her eyes.
"I'm going outside," she'd whisper over her shoulder,
and then went out to find her sister who,
Mother said, had been lost during the war.
"It doesn't matter
if I'll know who she is,"
she'd tell herself,
as she looked expectantly at the faces of strangers
waiting to be found,
"She'll recognize me."

AFTER THE WAR

I hold a picture of my mother
as a young girl
smiling on the grass in Sweden,
after the war.
I wonder where is the pain and sadness,
that I came to know
just a few years after,
did she fold them
like glasses
as she was photographed,
or that they came to her later on
when she held me,
looked into my eyes,
and called me by their names.

Testimony

My memories from Auschwitz began in the crib,
with a bottle that she propped against the side
so that she wouldn't have to hold me
as she busied herself with more important things.
Then the banishment to the backyard at age three when I dis-
      turbed the silence.
And so on through the years.
I have read all the books.
I have heard all the testimonies.
But when my turn came to tell our family's Holocaust story,
I could only remember the lonely boy in the yard.
I could only remember the disappointment in her eyes
as I told my memories from Auschwitz.

Stories of Apostasy
and Faith

THEOLOGY

One hundred and twenty-seven members of my family
were murdered in the Holocaust
not one of them deserved it.
So how do I see it?
There are two possibilities.
Either God was able to prevent their deaths
and chose not to,
despite the unwarrantedness,
then I see no reason
to thank him
or sing his praises.
Alternatively,
if God was helpless
incapable of coming to their aid,
then I don't have any reason
to be on his good side,
if he isn't any help.
But perhaps
I am misguided
so I pray from time to time
to keep in touch,
on the off chance
that my name will show on his caller ID
when I call.

Theology Chapter II

I sent my poem "Theology" to a friend
and he called me.
Listen—he says
there is another possibility,
that killing your family is not a cruel act
but God's positive deed
and you are simply incapable of understanding
his divine plan
which necessitated the death of your family.
I was silent for a second
then hung up, incensed,
and went to eat a whole bag of chips
never thinking that it was a salad.

GOD'S WRATH

God stays in his room,
and I'm in mine.
And because he does not eat,
he never goes to the kitchen.
And because he does not pee,
he never goes to the bathroom.
And because he doesn't need the air conditioner,
he doesn't sit with me in the living room.
And he knows everything
so doesn't sit with me to watch "60 Minutes."
When missiles fall,
he is in no danger
and he does not huddle next to me in the Safe Room.[36]
And on Shabbat, in the synagogue,
I look for him,
but cannot find him.
But I know that he exists
because, at night, he snores,
and keeps me awake.

---

36. Because of the constant threat of attack Israelis face, safe rooms have been mandated in all houses since 1992. They have to be bullet and fireproof with steel doors and sparse furnishings. They are sometimes called bomb shelters.

Nova[37]

God huddles behind a tree and weeps,
as Adam weaves between the trees.
The breeze carries Adam's cry
"Where art thou, my Lord"
and God answers
"I am naked
thus I must hide."

---

37. On October 7, 2023, attendees of the Nova Music Festival were the subject of the Hamas terror attack.

Curses and Blessings

At the bus stop he pointed at me in recognition
but I showed no assent.
Undaunted he came and shook my hand, his silver-framed
　　glasses askew.
"Let me finish my say then you can speak," he said.
"May God bless you three blessings
that you join in the building of the third Temple,[38]
that you live to see your children and grandchildren under
　　the wedding canopy
that all your enemies be vanquished."
I am mentally ill.
Please give me some 5 shekels so that Yehezkel in the
　　grocery
will give me a roll and a drink."
Which I did.
Some would dismiss this incident
but I chose to not.
You see, my mother stood on the frozen muddied ground
　　of Auschwitz,
whose cursed soil petrified generations of lives,
and I like to think that now God sends his peculiar
　　messengers
to bless me,

---

38. The third temple refers to a future rebuilding of the Temple in Jerusalem
after the destruction of the first and second temples there.

to warm my soul
and to spread his compassion
on the face of the earth.

Stories of Hope
and Healing

Farewells

I went to say goodbye to my parents
when they left the country.
My mother was busy the entire visit
packing up the leftovers
so I hardly had a chance to say goodbye.
"Hurry home before the dairy products spoil"
was the last thing she said as she closed the door.
I stood in the parking lot
laden with Tupperware,
feeling alone.
The next day I sat hunched over her reheated soup,
my hands encircled the bowl,
warming my fingers,
steam rising about my face,
as I waited for the soup to cool.
It has taken too much of a lifetime
to learn to live in a family
where you eat soup
instead of saying goodbye.

WHEN I GET OLDER

When I get older
I will start to try to remember
what my mother has chosen to forget.
But in the meantime
leave me to glean fragments of words and glances
and set them aside for later.

When I get older
I will start to build a legacy
out of the grey mists of the past.
But in the meantime
leave me commemorations
of disconcerting silence.

When I get older
I will buy pages gilded in gold
to write long and straight on vellum of ivory.
But in the meantime
leave me my scraps
on which to scrawl jagged sentences
that bend around stains and erasures.

When I get older,
I can start to imagine being someone
I hadn't imagined before
but in the meantime
leave me to sit on the park bench,

between my parents,
eating cream cheese sandwiches
out of waxed paper bags.

DREAMS

Everyone seems to have their lessons
from the Holocaust
except for me.
I only have the dead,
whom I try to extract
from my mother's nightmares
into my dreams.

A Birthday Present

God's gift for me on my birthday
was to be stuck on a bus,
for four hours and a half,
on the way to Jerusalem,
with the smell of burnt hay in the air.
Not a French eclair with vanilla custard,
not a private writing workshop with JD Salinger
but to be stranded next to a seven-year-old girl
who watched endless episodes of Peppa Pig
while snacking on Bamba peanut puffs.
I smelled the nutty fragrance,
and studied her little fingers
their tips tinged bright yellow
as I salivated in hunger.
To distract myself I turned my head forward, to the crawl of
    the cars ahead,
on their way to Jerusalem,
but the sweet smell of the Bamba
brought her back to my thoughts,
incessantly.
"Thou shalt not covet thy neighbor's wife."
But to covet the Bamba of your seven-year-old seatmate,
is that more or less forbidden?
What is sure to me is that if my seatmate had been
the wife of my neighbor
in actuality

this poem would never have been written.
God's gift for me on my birthday was a special seatmate.
At a quarter past nine we arrived at the bus station in
    Jerusalem,
and I went upstairs to catch an almost empty bus back home.
We drove without stopping
like prisoners, suddenly free,
distance themselves from confinement.
God gave me a gift for my birthday
a sense of liberation
and ruminations about all people
who suffered today on the way to Jerusalem
so that he could grant me a poem
for my birthday.

In Every Generation

In every generation, each person must see himself as if they left Egypt.—Haggadah[39]

In every generation a person must see
the light,
to guide his way in the darkness.
In every generation a person must hear
the whisper that has been silenced
and respond with tears.
In every generation a man must taste
the bitterness of existence
and he can learn to embrace.
In every generation, a person must smell
a scent of burnt expectations
and learn to mourn.
In every generation a person must learn to touch
and to be touched
and then he can impart.
In every generation a person must learn to dream
so that he can will himself to endure.

---

39. Haggadah is a Jewish text that sets out the rules and orders for Passover Seder.

Healing

If healing is the absence of pain
then there is no healing
because memory abounds
and every memory is tinged with pain.
Every hug I see reminds me of those I never felt
and every connection reminds me
of the attachment I never felt.
But perhaps there is healing amid the pain
a sadness that dims but does not extinguish
a pain that staggers but does not vanquish.
This too is healing
and I can do no more
and no less.

Afterword

A New Language
of Holocaust Remembrance—
From Trauma to Compassion

> *This lecture is about how the emotional and personal*
> *language that I utilized in my poetry was the trans-*
> *formative element in my construction of a meaningful*
> *Holocaust narrative of remembrance and in my process*
> *of healing the inherited trauma.*

The world of the Second Generation is a paradoxical one. The first paradox being, that, on the one hand, many of the Second Generation have been raised with little direct knowledge of the Holocaust. Our parents, in order to spare us the misery, hid from us the story of their suffering. But, despite this silence, we were also meant to serve as Memorial Candles, as the psychologist Dina Wardi termed it, children who were designated to memorialize those who died but who were never spoken of. This is a paradox of finding memory despite the silence. The second paradox regards our relationship with the survivor parent. My survivor parents were emotionally distant, unable to bond properly, and minimized physical contact with me. As a result, I have developed a fear of abandonment, suffer from low self-esteem, and lack basic trust. On the other hand, I felt valued and cherished as my parents' victory over Hitler and was subject to doting, parental worry and to extreme concern for my physical well-being and appearance.

93

I was raised in a jumble of conflicting emotions. This jumble of emotions made it difficult for me to compose a coherent life narrative. This is where poetry played an important role in helping me to find a path to develop a narrative of Holocaust remembrance and personal healing.

My path starts with confronting the repression of the traumatic memory surrounding the Holocaust:

It is hard for me to imagine that I had a family at all/I'm not a god that can create a family out of motes of dust ("Photographs," page 20).

My initial feeling is one of powerlessness when confronted with this repression of memory but also protest against it:

But a death unmourned/unnoted/is a cruelty that never should have been created ("Unknown/Unowned," page 18).

Yet, despite my parents' attempts to shield us from any memory of the Holocaust by never mentioning it, the Holocaust was an integral part of my identity:

An awareness that is never taught/can never be unlearned/ can never be forgotten ("Eclipse," page 17).

One aspect of this presence appears in my names. I knew I was named after my grandfather and was meant by this to commemorate him. In a way my life did not belong solely to me but also to him:

Names like the shadow that grew long/with the day's end./ Late that summer I would return to the tree/to pick these mulberries from the ground,/their sweetness bittered with dust,/ unaware of the names that had lodged in my soul/like the tiny hard seeds of a mulberry ("Berries," page 36).

The child of the survivor, being named after the dead relative, carries with him the burden of commemorating him. But

I knew nothing about him. How does one fill this role without any knowledge of the person?

They long to be mourned./But I, who have never known their embrace, cannot.../...It is a time of mourning/and I sit among the unmourned ("Unmourned," page 19).

Faced with the task of remembering what his parents chose to forget, each child of a survivor must find his or her own narrative memory (or repression) like the four sons of the Haggadah:

After the redemption there were four sons,/so too after the destruction ("Four Sons," page 32).

My own path was to create memory via poetry. Via the poetic language I was able to create a connection to my family from just a name or an image:

It is left for me to imagine my uncles crunching impatiently the hard candy when they tired of letting it dissolve,/as I would, a generation on ("Mints," page 29).

In my case, poetry served not only as an expression of the pain and longing, but also, a way to connect with those forgotten and to mourn them:

Like a latter-day Descartes,/"You were killed/therefore you were"/and I will grieve ("Ergo Sum," page 30).

The poetic imagination allowed me a connectedness to my family murdered during the Holocaust, thus enabling me to mourn and to process the traumatic memory.

In my initial poem "Photographs," I felt powerless in the face of the trauma, the poems "Names" and "Mints" allowed me to connect to those who were murdered. My poetry serves not only as an elegy for those murdered, but my own oath to mourning and processing the trauma.

The second role of poetry for me is allowing me the process of catharsis, to express the trauma inherent in being a child of Holocaust survivors. Because I believe the road to healing is to express these emotions, both negative and positive, I feel that my own personal development is furthered by my ability to express my feelings via poetry. Moreover, the poem is an effective way to express these feelings because its emotional language is able to describe the varying, often conflicting emotions in my life.

My parents married and had children immediately after the Holocaust, in the throes of trauma and it is clear to me they were not psychologically ready to raise a family:

Impelled by some impassive force of nature,/bent on renewal,/ to put forth these tiny, pale flowers/in the midst of the maelstrom ("Renewal," page 35).

In this poem, I am able to express both my anger at my parents for being emotionally unable to care for me properly while understanding their psychological need to rebuild their ruined world.

Another poem deals with the shared desire of the Second Generation to help the psychologically damaged parent by finding the Mother's child who was "lost" during the war:

As she looked expectantly at the faces of strangers/waiting to be found/"She'll recognize me" ("Missing Persons," page 72).

I felt that my Mother's love was conditional, that I needed to earn her love and that it was my own fault that I was not loved, that because of my behavior I was not worthy of love.

Once I was able to express these negative emotions, I could now start processing the pain and anger in order to touch my parents' warmth and love and the peculiar ways in which they were expressed:

It has taken too much of a lifetime/to learn to live in a

family/where you eat soup/instead of saying goodbye ("Farewells," page 85).

Thus, leading to a glimmer of hope and renewal:
When I get older/I will start to try to remember/what my mother has chosen to forget ("When I Get Older," page 86).

And the promise of healing:
And I like to think that now God sends his peculiar messengers/to bless me ("Curses and Blessings," page 81).

In conclusion, the poetic language provided me with a path to remembrance and mourning for those who have never been mourned and as a way to heal my intergenerational trauma. Poetry provided me with a new language of remembrance. This language by its very essence, emotional and personal, is a stark contrast to the traumatic and ideological language used in Holocaust remembrance and the remembrance of most collective trauma. The transformation of the language of memory to one both personal and emotional, has the potential to lead to healing and to help find resilience and strength from within the trauma:
To parse therewith a syntax of the pain,/then words entombed shall resurgent flow,/words whose tears may heal the soul again ("Ineffable," page 31).

It is my hope and dream that we all can transform our current pain and trauma into strength and resilience via the personal language of creativity, connectedness and compassion.